Just the Facts
# The Arms Trade
Richard Bingley

Heinemann
**LIBRARY**

# www.heinemann.co.uk/library
Visit our website to find out more information about **Heinemann Library** books.

To order:
- ☎ Phone 44 (0) 1865 888066
- 📄 Send a fax to 44 (0) 1865 314091
- 💻 Visit the Heinemann Bookshop at www.heinemann.co.uk/library to browse our catalogue and order online.

**Produced by Monkey Puzzle Media Ltd**
Gissing's Farm, Fressingfield, Suffolk IP21 5SH, UK

First published in Great Britain by Heinemann Library, Halley Court, Jordan Hill, Oxford OX2 8EJ, part of Harcourt Education.
Heinemann is a registered trademark of Harcourt Education Ltd.

Editorial: Isabel Thurston
Design: Mayer Media
Picture Research: Lynda Lines
Consultant: Gideon Burrows
Production: Viv Hichens

Originated by Dot Gradations Ltd
Printed and bound in Hong Kong, China by South China Printing Company

ISBN 0 431 16143 7
07 06 05 04 03
10 9 8 7 6 5 4 3 2 1

**British Library Cataloguing in Publication Data**
Bingley, Richard
The arms trade
382.4'56234
A full catalogue record for this book is available from the British Library.

**Acknowledgements**
The publishers would like to thank the following for permission to reproduce photographs:
Associated Press pp. 11 (Pavel Rahman), 25 (Adam Butler), 41 (Brennan Linsley); Corbis pp. 18, 28 (Bettman), 29 (Bettman), 31 (Robert Patrick/Sygma); Corbis Digital Stock p. 40 (Bud Freund); Defence Picture Library p. 36–37; Digital Vision pp. 4, 16; Peter Newark's Pictures pp. 14–15, 30; Popperfoto pp. 5 (Reuters), 7 (Reuters), 20 (Reuters) 22–23 (Reuters), 44 (Reuters), 46–47 (Reuters); Rex Features pp. 33 (David Hartley), 43 (Mark Peters); Still Pictures pp. 38–39 (Mark Edwards), 45 (Carlos Guarita), 51 (Gary Trotter); Topham Picturepoint pp. 13 (AP), 14, 17, 19, 35; TRH Pictures pp. 6, 9, 12, 16 (IWM), 26, 48–49.

Cover photograph reproduced with permission of Topham Picturepoint.

Every effort has been made to contact copyright holders of any material reproduced in this book. Any omissions will be rectified in subsequent printings if notice is given to the publishers.

Any words appearing in the text in bold, **like this**, are explained in the Glossary.

# Contents

# Introduction

The arms trade is an **industry**, like any other. Just as some companies produce food or materials to sell abroad, others sell arms. The arms trade covers the buying and selling of weapons systems; arms sales are often referred to as defence **exports**. Arms can range from small pistols up to high-tech jet aircraft or military computers. Also included in the trade are weapon **components**, such as electronics.

Many industries have both good and bad effects at the same time. Nuclear power, for example, is a way to generate huge amounts of electricity for our homes, but it can also be used to make bombs that could destroy the world. The arms trade creates similar difficulties. Arms have helped countries and individuals defend themselves against aggression; but there are countless occasions where weapons have been used to terrorize defenceless communities.

The F-18 Hornet fighter aircraft, made in the USA by McDonnell Douglas (part of Boeing) has been sold to Australia, Canada, Finland, Kuwait, Malaysia, Spain and Switzerland. Each plane costs US$ 7 million to make.

This book examines the different ways the arms trade operates, and traces the history of the trade. The issues around the arms trade have always provoked strong emotions – from disapproval to praise – and they affect today's world more than ever.

Towards the end, the book summarizes the arguments for and against the selling of arms. It is important to debate the issues, and ask what is good and what is bad about the trade.

A US soldier secures the area during the arrival of troops near Kabul, Afghanistan, as part of international peacekeeping forces.

# What is the arms trade?

Arms are bought mainly by three groups of people: governments – known as **state actors** – whose countries may not produce adequate equipment to defend themselves or launch military operations; **non-state actors,** who are usually groups committed to overthrowing governments; and criminals, who want to seize money, property or people.

## Legal trade

Nowadays, most of the arms trade is **legal** and takes place publicly between different countries. Each country has a slightly different set of legal rules, but most governments who allow arms to be sold abroad (by granting **export licences**)

say that their arms **exports** should not be used for unprovoked aggression. They should also not be used against the country that sells them.

There are many cases where such rules seem to have been ignored. Many people criticize the legal trade, because arms are sometimes sold to countries with brutal or aggressive regimes. Yet defence exporters point out that they do not know beforehand how arms will be used, and that these cases are exceptional rather than normal.

Illegally traded weapons are often small arms, such as this double action pistol, which are easy to conceal.

# Illegal trade

Just as in other trades, arms selling is sometimes undertaken illegally. This may be done by people who support a particular cause where a minority is fighting against an armed state, or by people wishing to profit from the situation in troubled areas.

It is difficult to steal a warship or a jet fighter, so illegal arms tend to be small arms such as pistols, rifles, machine guns and even mortar bombs. These are portable, easy to smuggle and hide, and cheap enough to sell quickly.

Indonesian customs officer with confiscated arms.

7

# The legal arms trade

Arms are sold **legally** from two main sources – government defence ministries and private or state-owned companies.

A defence ministry is a government department responsible for the country's armed forces and military equipment. When a defence ministry buys new equipment, or has a **surplus**, it will sometimes sell older weapons abroad. The **reunification** of Germany is a good example.

After the Second World War, Germany was split into two separate countries – East and West Germany. In 1990 they were reunified into one country and needed only one army and navy. The East German naval fleet was sold to Indonesia.

In 2001, Germany's defence ministry offered second-hand arms – including mortar bombs, fighter planes, tanks and submarines – to an approved list of 50 countries that had friendly relations with Germany.

Private or state-owned companies will usually sell both to the home country's defence ministry and abroad. Orders from abroad help keep the production lines running if the home country's needs are not high. The large value of such exports is one reason why the arms trade is seen as different to other businesses.

Super Lynx helicopter made by GKN–Westland in the UK.

Many jobs depend on winning one large contract; in this case senior politicians, such as the British and Swedish prime ministers, visited South Africa to support bids from their countries. Due to the enormous pressure to win such important contracts, there also tend to be more allegations of **'sweeteners'** in the arms trade than in other business practices. This means that governments and suppliers negotiate arms deals using offers of rewards or even bribes. Over forty allegations of this kind were reported in the two years following the South African deal.

# Case study  South Africa

The South African government agreed to spend US$ 4 billion on arms in 1999.
Their home defence industry was unable to produce the equipment they needed,
and they purchased the following arms.

| Equipment | Production company and country |
| --- | --- |
| 28 fighter jets | BAE Systems-SAAB (UK and Sweden) |
| 24 fighter trainer jets | BAE Systems-SAAB (UK and Sweden) |
| 30 light helicopters | Agusta (Italy) |
| 3 submarines | German Submarine Consortium (Germany) |
| 4 Lynx helicopters | GKN-Westland (UK) |

# The illegal arms trade

The illegal arms trade is sometimes referred to as the illicit trade, which means it is forbidden. Most illegally or illicitly traded arms tend to be pistols, rifles, machine guns and even portable anti-tank and aircraft missile systems.

## Where do illegal arms come from?

One of the main sources is former war zones. Large amounts of weaponry are circulated during **conflict**, and controls over equipment have usually totally broken down because of the confusion of war. At the end of the conflict many of these weapons remain hoarded by groups for future use; they may later seek to sell them. The 1990s Balkan wars, in the former Republic of Yugoslavia, led to floods of small arms entering European cities.

In some countries gun ownership is more widely permitted than others, so arms can be bought there, and illegally shipped abroad to areas and groups prohibited from receiving **legal** arms sales, perhaps by a **United Nations (UN) embargo** – an order to stop the transfer of arms into a country.

Other illegally traded weapons may be stolen from armed forces and police bases around the world. For example, in Australia in 1998, hundreds of assault rifles, grenades, anti-tank mines and rocket launchers went missing from army bases. In communities where guns are more widely allowed, gun shops are raided too.

Most arms start out being legally produced and shipped, but may then be **diverted** before reaching their stated destination. In 1999, Polish tanks disappeared after they were officially sold to Yemen. They were reportedly delivered to Sudan, which was under a UN arms embargo at the time.

Many states allow arms to be exported to other countries, but have weak **export** controls. This is a particular problem in poorer countries, which desperately need the money from arms sales.

In certain situations, governments support groups or countries secretly by arming them (see Afghanistan case study on page 12). This is not always illegal in the supplier country, but often feeds illegal arms sales in the recipient country, as arms are often hoarded by unofficial groups (rebels) who can sell or use them at a later date.

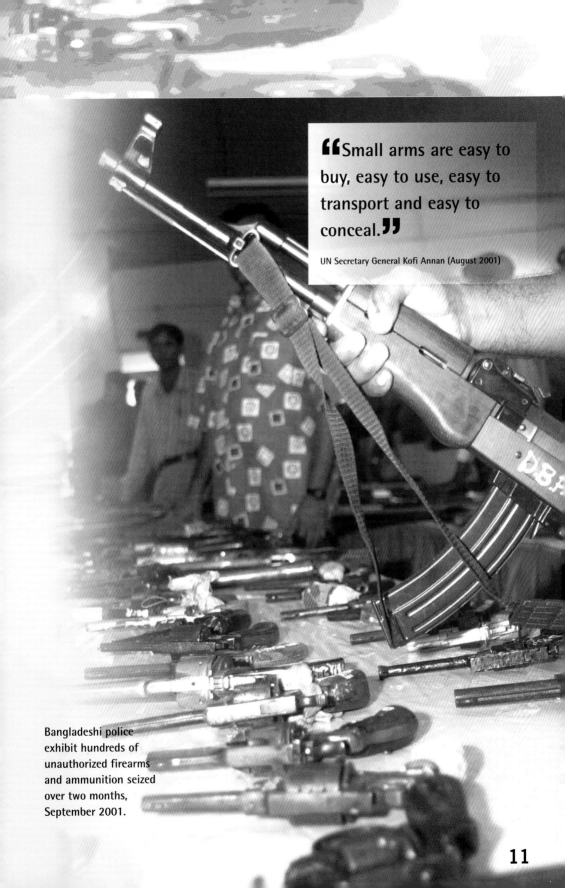

**❝Small arms are easy to buy, easy to use, easy to transport and easy to conceal.❞**

UN Secretary General Kofi Annan (August 2001)

Bangladeshi police exhibit hundreds of unauthorized firearms and ammunition seized over two months, September 2001.

11

# Case study: Afghanistan

US Army Stinger.

In 1979 the Soviet Union sent troops into the country to defend the new communist government. When they withdrew ten years later, they had spent US$ 70 billion and lost 14,000 troops. At this time, the two **superpowers**, the USA and the Soviet Union, led the '**Cold War**'. The USA was worried about what the Soviet Union was doing in Afghanistan, but did not want to risk entering the war directly. Instead, throughout the 1980s it supported the Afghan rebels fighting Soviet troops, with arms and training. The most famous piece of equipment was the Stinger, a shoulder-held missile launcher, which terrorized Soviet helicopter pilots.

Afghanistan is a strongly Muslim country. In the 1970s the **Soviet Union** was ruled by a **communist** government, which wanted to spread communist ideas. Soviet-supported communists seized power in Afghanistan in 1978, provoking revolts by the Afghan people, led by the Mujahideen ('holy warriors').

Stingers are credited with tipping the balance in favour of the Mujahideen.

After the end of Soviet occupation, the USA became worried that Stingers would be sold abroad, and attempted to buy them back. However, by that time many had been hidden by local Afghan groups or sold abroad illegally. This is a good example of how arms can create safety in one instance and danger the next.

Soviet troops in Afghanistan, 1988.

# The origins of the arms trade

Arms trading can be traced back to the 14th century with the introduction of gunpowder in Europe. Markets for powder-charged weapons grew as armies demanded canons and firearms. Arms production as an **industry** – where weapons were made on a large scale for trading – first grew in Liège, Belgium.

In the industrial revolution, during the late 18th and 19th centuries, weapons technology advanced quickly. Armies were forced to acquire new equipment before it became outdated. Many countries had larger armies than before. When France attacked Russia in 1812, Napoleon used half a million soldiers – twenty times the size of previous European forces.

Hiram Maxim with his invention, the first machine gun.

Throughout the 19th century, legendary arms industries emerged. Aged fourteen, Alfred Krupp inherited his father's steel company, and turned increasingly to making armaments. Half of Krupp's guns were sold outside his native Prussia – now part of Germany – and he established a worldwide reputation as the 'Cannon King'. In 1866 Austria and Prussia were at war and Krupp sold guns to both sides. Questions over loyalty have always blighted arms executives. Krupp died in 1887, employing 20,000 workers and owning the world's largest arms company.

In the UK, Vickers built warships and sold a new type of gun – the Maxim machine gun. Vickers employed Basil Zaharoff, whose life reads like a movie script. He won orders around the world, which enabled him to marry a Spanish duchess and buy mansions in Paris and Monte Carlo. In the north of England lay the vast factories of Armstrong, which made rifles, ships and submarines for Italy, Egypt, Turkey, Chile and the USA. In the USA a company called Du Pont supplied gunpowder to Spain and anti-Spanish rebels in Latin America, and armed both Russia and the UK in the Crimean War (1854).

By the end of the 19th century the major arms companies had agents around the world, mixing with politicians, generals and royalty. Machine guns and warships now replaced the medieval technology of pistols and cannons. The trade was a leading industry, and had become truly international.

70-tonne naval gun leaving the Krupp workshops in Essen, 1914.

# World at war

Arms traders, who had come to represent modern industrial progress, were at the same time using countries' fears to increase their orders. Arms dealers such as Basil Zaharoff exploited tensions between governments – for example, where neighbouring countries were hostile and frightened of attack from others. Once he sold Greece a submarine, and frightened its neighbour, Turkey, into buying two. He then alarmed the Russians with tales of danger from the south, and **Tsar** Nicholas II bought four submarines.

The First World War (1914–18) increased arms production. Profits for the trade soared, as so much equipment was needed. However, the war was disastrous for the image of the

First World War trenches.

**industry**. In one instance, in the battle of the Dardanelles, the Germans used British-made guns that had been sold by Zaharoff before war broke out, against British troops.

Aircraft, like this Spitfire, became a major part of the arms trade in the 20th century.

The League of Nations was established in 1919 after the First World War, to promote international cooperation. The League adopted a covenant including six 'grave objections' to arms companies, accusing them of playing off one country against another. By the time of the Second World War, however, the League of Nations was no longer effective as an organization.

Other attempts to control the trade continued. In 1932 an international **disarmament** conference was held in Geneva. In the USA, the Nye Committee investigated effects of the arms trade. This resulted in the formation of the Munitions Control Board, which governed US arms sales, and tried to ensure they did not end up in undesirable places – such as war zones. In the UK, Labour Party politicians called for arms factories to be owned by government. If government owned the arms factories they could ensure equipment was not sold to potential enemies.

However, the world changed dramatically during this time. Japanese expansion into China, and Hitler's re-armament of German troops with Krupp-made battleships and tanks, provoked worldwide concern. The Second World War (1939–45) provided a spectacular change of fortune for the image of arms manufacturers. British Spitfire fighter planes made by Vickers Supermarine, and Hawker Hurricanes, defeated Germany's Messerschmitt fighter aircraft in the Battle of Britain (1940). A massive aerospace industry grew in the USA, headed by Lockheed Martin and Boeing. This provided the allied forces against Hitler with bombers – such as Lockheed's Hudson and Boeing's Flying Fortress. The industry was celebrated by the victors for playing an important part in defending countries against aggression. In the USA a military super-industry had grown, which was to lead the world arms trade until today – and beyond.

# The Cold War 1945–91

President John F Kennedy during the
Cuban Missile Crisis, 1962.

For the next 50 years much of the world split into two opposing camps – led by the two '**superpowers**', the **Soviet Union** on one side and the USA on the other. Although the two countries resisted direct war, a threatening mood – known as the **Cold War** – provoked arms production and sales.

The Soviets offered military aid, including arms, to 'wars of liberation' – groups or governments working to overthrow the interests of the USA or its allies. Similarly, the USA pledged to support any organization fighting **communist** expansion. In Latin America alone, the USA sent arms to El Salvador, Honduras, Argentina, Paraguay and Venezuela. The Soviet Union attempted to counter US influence in the region, and sent arms to Cuba, Nicaragua and Peru.

Most arms deals during this period were an attempt by one superpower to reduce the power of the other. Arms supplies were principally used as tools to draw countries into, or away from, **alliances** led by the USA or the Soviet Union. Friendly countries or political groups were rewarded with arms for their support. The USA built **alliances** because they feared communist ideas might spread and take over in their own country. The Soviet Union, equally, found the USA's worldwide influence threatening, and tried to reduce US power by forming alliances.

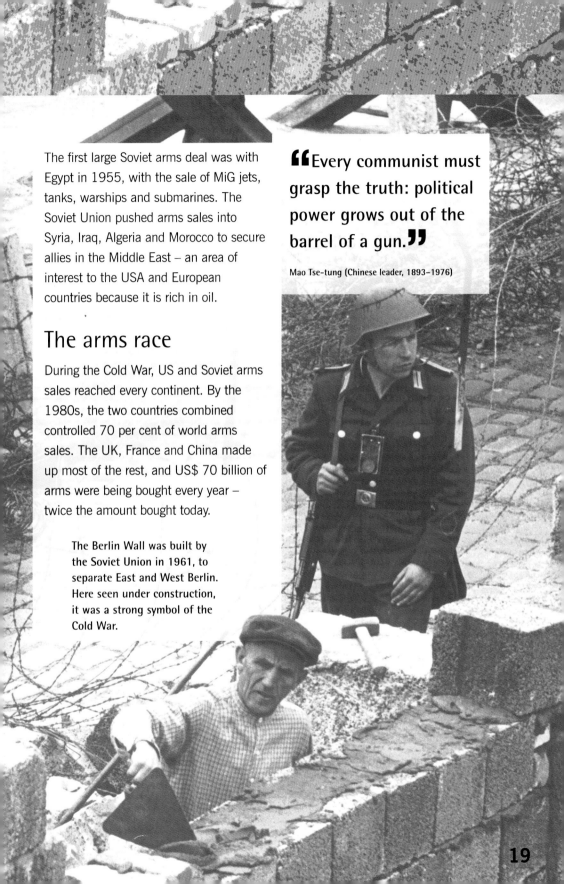

The first large Soviet arms deal was with Egypt in 1955, with the sale of MiG jets, tanks, warships and submarines. The Soviet Union pushed arms sales into Syria, Iraq, Algeria and Morocco to secure allies in the Middle East – an area of interest to the USA and European countries because it is rich in oil.

## The arms race

During the Cold War, US and Soviet arms sales reached every continent. By the 1980s, the two countries combined controlled 70 per cent of world arms sales. The UK, France and China made up most of the rest, and US$ 70 billion of arms were being bought every year – twice the amount bought today.

**66**Every communist must grasp the truth: political power grows out of the barrel of a gun.**99**

Mao Tse-tung (Chinese leader, 1893–1976)

The Berlin Wall was built by the Soviet Union in 1961, to separate East and West Berlin. Here seen under construction, it was a strong symbol of the Cold War.

# Post-Cold War

Democracy swept through Eastern Europe in the late 1980s, and the **Soviet Union** collapsed in 1991. The Soviet leadership, which had kept the individual states together in opposition to the West, was replaced by a more open approach and the beginnings of reform. The major part of the former Soviet Union became known as Russia. With the USA and Russia no longer in open opposition, much of the world felt safer. However, large stocks of weapons existed; many of which would be sold around the world over the years that followed.

Defence exporters had to look for new markets during the 1990s as arms purchasing programmes in Europe, Russia and the USA shrank due to the new, safer climate. Developing countries of Asia and the Middle East now became the focus of most arms sales. The main reason for sales in these regions is that they contain areas of grave tension. China and Taiwan, the Korean peninsula,

United Arab Emirates Airforce staff look over a South African built Skua high speed target drone, during the biggest Middle East Arms Show, Abu Dhabi, March 1999.

Israel and the Palestinian territories and India and Pakistan are all areas where **arms races** often spring up. This is because of strong religious, ethnic or political divides, which often have a long history. For example, the current conflict between India and Pakistan over Kashmir began as long ago as 1947. India is a mainly Hindu country, but is tolerant of other religions, while Pakistan is strongly Muslim. In 1947, the Maharaja (ruler) of Kashmir, fearing internal tribal warfare, opted to join India.

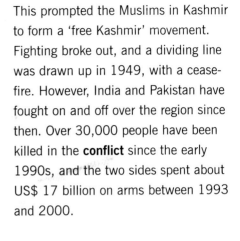

This prompted the Muslims in Kashmir to form a 'free Kashmir' movement. Fighting broke out, and a dividing line was drawn up in 1949, with a cease-fire. However, India and Pakistan have fought on and off over the region since then. Over 30,000 people have been killed in the **conflict** since the early 1990s, and the two sides spent about US$ 17 billion on arms between 1993 and 2000.

The arms trade remains strong because some parts of the world are still unsafe. Around thirty wars were raging every year during the 1990s. Conflicts feed demand for arms. Some argue the **Cold War** kept a lid on many potentially large conflicts, because the consequences of the USA and the Soviet Union being drawn into direct confrontation would have been too damaging to entertain. This could even have ended in a nuclear **holocaust**.

The legal arms trade has almost halved in value since Cold War times, but it is still a huge global business (almost 1 per cent of world trade). With the strict **alliances** gone, countries may sell arms to most state customers without displeasing a **superpower**. A more open arms market has resulted, shaped by economic **globalization**.

**21**

# Small arms

Half a million people are killed annually by small arms. Most are **civilians** – not soldiers involved in war. The impact of small arms appears worse than any other sector of the arms trade. The trade is worth around US$ 5 billion per year, which is about 10 per cent of the entire global trade.

The number of countries producing small arms has grown dramatically. Nowadays, they are **legally** made in 95 countries – half the nations on earth. New production adds to the large volume of guns that flooded into many **developing countries** before 1991. The large number of small arms means they are the least controlled part of the trade.

The result is that over 500 million guns are in circulation today – one for every twelve people on earth. Firearms are extremely cheap in many areas: the UK charity Oxfam reported Kalashnikov rifles being sold for the price of a chicken in Sudan.

The use of small arms in war zones presents difficulties, especially for young people. Millions every year experience the death of family members, as well as learning difficulties, ejection from home and long-term ill health and disability – all caused by the unsettled conditions of life. It is estimated that four out of ten civilian casualties in **conflict** are under eighteen years old. Furthermore, there are about

300,000 child soldiers around the world – they are useful because they are agile, fast and obedient. The international community is concerned that more and more children are living in cultures of violence, where the only way to settle a dispute is with a gun, rather than through understanding and dialogue.

Small arms also pose dangers to rebuilding communities after war. Immediately after conflict, living essentials are often scarce, and structures of law and order may have broken down. Armed gangs or political groups sometimes believe they can get more resources through armed violence than they can by following peaceful channels.

Because small weapons are more widely available they are more widely used – whether by African cattle rustlers or criminal gangs in cities around the world. Such problems feed a feeling of terror; demand for guns grows as people seek to protect themselves.

Solving problems associated with small arms trading has therefore become an increasing priority for international organizations such as the **UN** (see pages 37–38).

**❝Small arms have been the basic method of mass killing over the past decade.❞**

Robin Cook (British Foreign Secretary 1997-2001)

A local village 'defence committee' in Banihal, India, 2001.

# Case study: Conflict diamonds

Sierra Leone in West Africa has been devastated by civil war between Revolutionary United Front (RUF) rebels and government forces. The country is rich in diamond reserves, and in 1990 RUF forces seized control of diamond mining territories.

The RUF sold diamonds, making money to pay for arms. Hence the phrase '**conflict** diamonds'. The RUF is known as one of the most brutal rebel groups, commonly amputating victims' limbs, and forcing children into combat.

The **UN** introduced arms **embargoes** and asked diamond-trading nations to ensure conflict diamonds were not sold in their shops. Despite UN requests, arms supplies to RUF forces continued. Planeloads of rifles, machine guns, rocket grenades and missiles came from the Ukraine into Burkina Faso, a country next to Sierra Leone. The UN reported that arms from other former Soviet and Eastern European countries were flown to Burkina Faso – then transferred to the RUF in Sierra Leone. The Burkina Faso government was paid in diamonds.

RUF diamonds were also passed into Liberia, another neighbour, in exchange for arms and military training. Sierra Leone's government faced difficulty coping with the wealthy RUF. Many government soldiers were disloyal, and the government relied on private security companies to protect diamond and oil reserves. Many of these companies have also been criticized for breaking arms embargoes and buying weapons. Companies caught breaking embargoes can have their directors prosecuted under domestic law. Countries that break embargoes can be placed under diplomatic or economic **sanctions** – although this happens only rarely.

A fourteen-year-old soldier holds a British rifle while patrolling the small town of Ropath in Sierra Leone.

In the late 1990s, the UN sent 8000 peacekeeping troops to Sierra Leone, but 300 were seized by the RUF. Overall the growth of small arms has lead to the slaughter of thousands of innocent **civilians** in Sierra Leone. But diamond selling, which makes people a lot of money, stretches beyond the borders of Sierra Leone. The UN reported that 'conflict' diamonds had ended up in the large diamond markets of Europe. World-wide conflict diamond trading is worth US$ 3–7 billion a year. Much of this money is used to buy guns in Africa, helping to make this type of arms trading very difficult to manage.

# Conventional weapons

The **UN** defines larger conventional weapons as: battle tanks; combat vehicles; large-calibre artillery systems; combat aircraft; attack helicopters; warships; missiles and missile launchers.

Conventional equipment costs much more than small arms. A US F-16 fighter jet costs Lockheed Martin around US$ 27 million to make. Conventional arms account for over 80 per cent of the world arms trade.

Here are some examples with their countries of origin:

Tanks:    T-90 (Russia); Challenger 2 (UK); M1 Abrams (USA)

Aircraft:   F-16 (USA) speed 2400kph; MiG-21 (Russia and China) speed 2100kph; Mirage 2000 (France) speed 2650kph

Missiles:  Tomahawk (USA): speed 900kph; Exocet (France) speed 1100kph

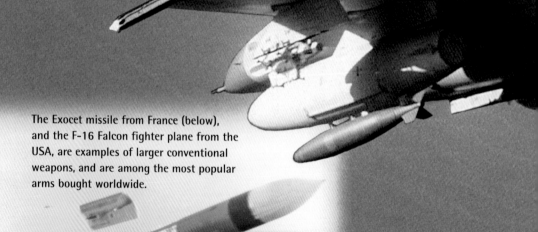

The Exocet missile from France (below), and the F-16 Falcon fighter plane from the USA, are examples of larger conventional weapons, and are among the most popular arms bought worldwide.

All these items are for sale. The F-16 is sold extensively around the world, especially in the Middle East. The MiG-21 is used in 47 countries, whilst the Mirage 2000 is available in seven. Exocet missiles are found in thirteen countries including Iraq, whilst Challenger tanks roam the Middle East.

Although many countries are careful not to sell the latest equipment to states that may attack them, sometimes buyers transfer arms to states where they were not originally intended to go. Recently Saudi Arabia was criticized for selling American missile technology on to China.

The UN estimates that 119 of the world's 198 states are involved in conventional arms sales – either as buyers or sellers. Large arms are now spread around the world in more areas than ever, so there is less overall control over the trade than ever before.

Some argue the world has become more dangerous, as large arms can more easily fall into the wrong hands. However, many arms producers say the spread of larger weapons has deterred large-scale conflict.

**❝It's important to remember the world is already awash in weapons systems...this can have a major impact on planning for peacekeeping operations.❞**

Lt. General James R Clapper, Director of the Defense Intelligence Agency (1995)

# Weapons of mass destruction

In 1948 the **UN** introduced a new category of arms called Weapons of Mass Destruction: this included atomic explosives, radioactive material weapons (such as bombs made from uranium or plutonium, which emit energy, causing illness or death to people over-exposed to it), chemical and biological weapons.

## Nuclear weapons

During the Second World War, the USA, the UK and the **Soviet Union** feared the German leader, Adolf Hitler, was developing an atom bomb – after two German scientists demonstrated nuclear fission in 1938 by splitting atoms to create powerful explosions. Hitler thought that if he developed an atomic bomb, hundreds of times more dangerous than other explosives at the time, important military powers would be too scared to defend themselves against Germany. In fact, it was the top-secret US 'Manhattan Project' that succeeded in exploding the first atomic weapon.

A scarred child survivor from Hiroshima sits in a destroyed schoolroom.

## Declared nuclear weapons states:

USA (1945)
Soviet Union, now Russia (1949)
Britain (1952)    France (1960)
China (1964)    India (1998)
Pakistan (1998)

## Undeclared:

Israel

('Undeclared' means that Israel has nuclear weapons capability but has not publicly declared it.)

## Suspected to be developing nuclear weapons:

Iraq    Iran    North Korea

In 1945, allied forces dropped atom bombs on Hiroshima and Nagasaki in Japan. About 67,000 people perished within the first day and a further 36,000 by the end of the year – due to injuries and the effects of radiation. This remains the only time atom bombs have been used in warfare. Most countries treat nuclear weapons with extreme caution now they know the devastation they can cause.

From the 1960s, international agreements have been made to stop nuclear arms spreading. However, there are reports of scientists moving to states seeking to develop nuclear weapons, and of materials being moved illegally. This has been a grave concern since Russia's huge nuclear arsenal became poorly guarded and funded after the end of the **Cold War**. After the collapse of the Soviet Union, the Russian government had many pressing worries, as the country's **industry** and economy were severely shaken.

Another problem is that much equipment needed to make weapons is also used for peaceful projects: this is known as **dual-use**. Canada supplied reactors for Pakistan's nuclear energy power stations and the USA did the same for India. Instead, both countries reportedly used the radioactive material in the reactors to develop nuclear weaponry.

Because of strict controls there is little legal nuclear arms trading. Any sale of technology tends to be secret and illegal. Nuclear arms sales, therefore, make up a tiny fraction of the arms trade.

Hiroshima, Japan, was devastated by the atom bomb in 1945.

# Chemical and biological weapons

Some weapons are made from deadly chemicals or bacteria and are designed to poison, choke or burn people. These are called chemical and biological weapons (CBW), and are almost impossible to trace within the arms trade because they can be made from everyday products such as cleaning fluids.

CBW are hardly a modern device of warfare. The ancient Assyrians and Persians poisoned drinking water, and the Romans used smoke to choke their enemies. In the 14th century an army besieging the Crimean port of Kaffa catapulted plague-infected human bodies over the city walls.

In the First World War, the French used tear gas and Germany used chlorine – a green-coloured gas designed to choke the enemy. Chlorine was readily available as a low-cost industrial product and is more commonly used as a cleaning fluid, especially in swimming pools. Gas masks were soon introduced to reduce the impact of these attacks.

Despite the Geneva Protocol in 1925, which outlawed the use of chemical and biological weapons in war, continuing conflicts and the **Cold War** inspired more dangerous inventions, such as Tabun and mustard gas, and VX gas. Tabun and VX are known as 'nerve agents' because they attack the body's nervous system, causing paralysis and breathing difficulties. Mustard gas burns any exposed skin, lungs and eyes. Later, scandals erupted in Germany as German companies – innocently, they argued – provided Iraq with chemicals it was able to turn against Iran and Kurdish communities in the 1980s.

Machine gun crew on the Somme during WWI, 1916, wearing gas masks.

When **UN** weapons inspectors went into Iraq after the Gulf War (1990–91) between Iraq and a US-led coalition, they located biological weapons facilities. The use of biological weapons is also known as 'germ warfare'. Germs, such as Anthrax, were being grown as cultures for possible use as weapons.

At least twenty states have had chemical and biological weapons programmes. Russia reportedly holds the largest CBW stockpile, built up when it was part of the **Soviet Union** (1922–91). It is very difficult to stop products such as chlorine or fly-spray being traded. This part of the arms trade, more than any other, demonstrates the difficulty of establishing how equipment sold abroad will be used.

> **"The greatest threat to life on earth is weapons of mass destruction – nuclear, chemical, biological."**
>
> Richard Butler (Head of UN Special Commission on Iraq, 1997–99)

A Kurdish victim of chemical warfare in Iraq.

# Globalization

**Globalization** is when production and sales move beyond national boundaries and operate within a 'borderless' world. Globalization has increased in the arms trade since the strict **alliances** of the **Cold War** ceased to operate. Free trade (international trade without restrictions) agreements and global communication systems such as the Internet have also helped.

## How is the arms trade becoming global?

National boundaries are becoming increasingly unimportant with the growth of international trade agreements. In Europe and the USA, moves have been made to introduce free trade agreements for arms trading, which will also involve Australia and Japan. Defence **exports** will be shipped to friendly nations without specific permission being needed for each **component** or project.

In order to become bigger and more competitive, one company often joins with, or purchases another. These mergers are increasingly international. According to **SIPRI** (the Stockholm International Peace Research Institute), 59 arms companies were acquired by European and US defence companies alone between 1998 and 1999. A prime example was French electronics giant Thomson-CSF buying Australian Defence Industries.

Companies from different countries also form partnerships because by sharing technologies they make a better end product. This is why arms manufacturers particularly want free trade agreements. For example, making the Challenger 2 tank – manufactured in the UK – involves 250 smaller companies that all contribute to the overall product, some of whom are based abroad.

Companies sometimes allow foreign companies to make their product, under a licensed production agreement. This is an increasingly popular arrangement with those buying arms, because they can assemble the equipment in their own country – generating jobs at home. A recent SIPRI report showed fourteen countries, including Australia, the USA and the UK, license arms production across 46 other countries.

Globalization in the arms trade has created controversy because many people claim controls over the sale of weapons are becoming fewer, when they are needed more than ever before. Arms manufacturers say that globalization speeds up and improves production, and creates a more open and safe world, where countries depend more on each other.

## Fact box

Saab (Sweden) and BAE Systems (UK) are huge aircraft manufacturers in their own right but recently teamed up to form Gripen International – an **alliance** that sells fighter jets and has secured contracts in South Africa and the Czech Republic.

The Challenger 2 tank is produced in the UK, using 250 international manufacturers to make different parts.

# Popular culture

Films, books, newspapers and television are important sources of information. The ways in which subjects such as the arms trade are covered tend to shape our opinions.

Large legal arms sales, like any other business, usually register on financial and foreign pages in more serious newspapers, whereas arms scandals and illegal activities have a higher profile. This tends to be the same for television and radio news bulletins.

However, due to high-profile campaigns, awareness of the arms trade is increasing. An international campaign to ban landmines was backed by Princess Diana, who visited the former war zones of Angola and Bosnia where many of these bombs lie buried. Followed by media photographers and broadcasters, she was able to show the world amputees who had lost their limbs while going about their normal daily lives, sometimes many years after wars had ended.

In 2002 other arms sales also received international publicity as India and Pakistan almost came to war over the disputed territory of Kashmir. Both sides were armed with nuclear weapons, and had spent billions of dollars on arms supplied from the US, the UK, China, France, Russia and Israel. There was great public fear that the consequences of such a huge war would create dangers in other countries.

**"How can countries which manufacture and trade in these weapons square their conscience with such human devastation?"**

Princess Diana (1961-1997), speaking to the Mines Advisory Group and Landmines Survivors Network, 1997

The James Bond movie *Tomorrow Never Dies* (1997), starring Pierce Brosnan, opens spectacularly on the Russian border at a shadowy snow-drenched arms bazaar. Bond destroys the bazaar before taking off in a fighter-plane armed with nuclear torpedoes, pursued by MiG jets. This shows a highly glamorized view of the arms trade.

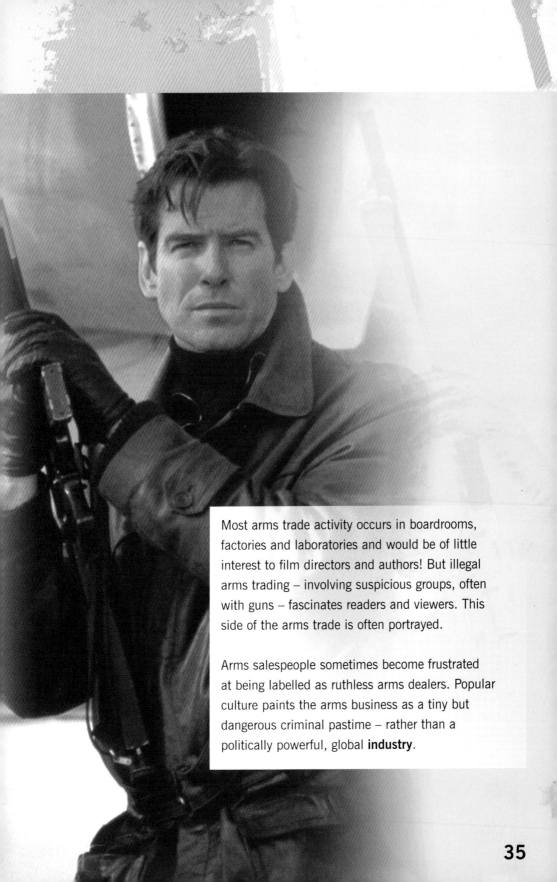

Most arms trade activity occurs in boardrooms, factories and laboratories and would be of little interest to film directors and authors! But illegal arms trading – involving suspicious groups, often with guns – fascinates readers and viewers. This side of the arms trade is often portrayed.

Arms salespeople sometimes become frustrated at being labelled as ruthless arms dealers. Popular culture paints the arms business as a tiny but dangerous criminal pastime – rather than a politically powerful, global **industry**.

# Arguments for the arms trade

Although most people individually do not want wars to happen, sadly it is inevitable that they will happen in some form. As long as there are wars, the demand for weapons will sustain an arms trade.

## Suppliers' arguments

The trade provides employment, often in highly skilled jobs. Around 500,000 people work for the world's ten largest arms companies. Many communities rely on arms production as the local source of employment. The trade is seen as a useful way for governments to balance their country's finances. Countries always try to reduce the gap between the amount they **import** and the amount they sell abroad.

Making arms for foreign customers keeps production lines running when orders from home are scarce, and enables technological progress to continue. Such progress will benefit armed services at home, because they will get improved weapons systems.

In the right hands, arms can be used to good effect, to keep order and as a deterrent to crime.

**"Weapons are not the problem, it is the men behind them."**

Gerald Bull (Canadian Artillery and Rocket Manufacturer, 1928-1990)

Warrior armed personnel carriers, produced in the UK by GKN, waiting outside the factory to be loaded aboard ships for transport.

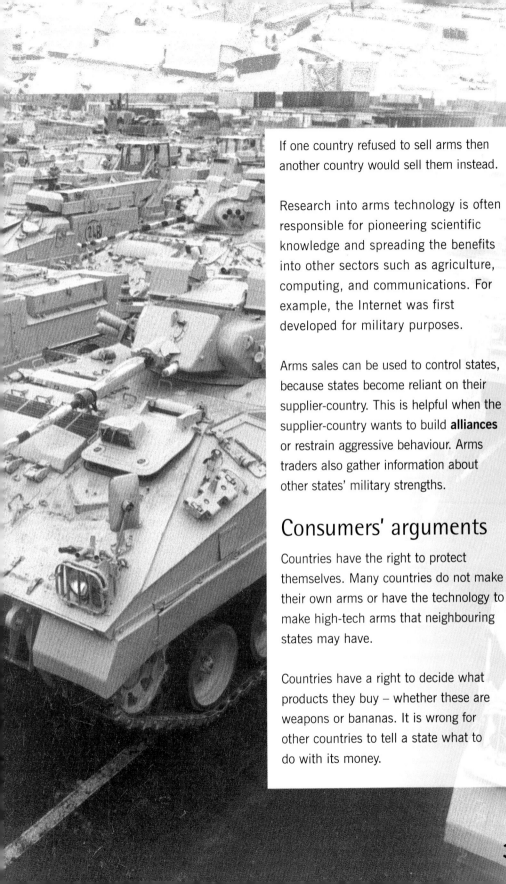

If one country refused to sell arms then another country would sell them instead.

Research into arms technology is often responsible for pioneering scientific knowledge and spreading the benefits into other sectors such as agriculture, computing, and communications. For example, the Internet was first developed for military purposes.

Arms sales can be used to control states, because states become reliant on their supplier-country. This is helpful when the supplier-country wants to build **alliances** or restrain aggressive behaviour. Arms traders also gather information about other states' military strengths.

## Consumers' arguments

Countries have the right to protect themselves. Many countries do not make their own arms or have the technology to make high-tech arms that neighbouring states may have.

Countries have a right to decide what products they buy – whether these are weapons or bananas. It is wrong for other countries to tell a state what to do with its money.

# Arguments against the arms trade

Arms are sometimes deliberately sold into areas of **conflict** and tension. The more countries or **non-state actors** become armed, the easier it is for them to be drawn away from peaceful solutions towards the use of weapons. In this way, the arms trade does not increase our security, but reduces it.

Arms have often been used against soldiers from the countries that sold them in the first place. In the Gulf War, French troops faced attack from Iraqi air forces with Mirage jets, made in France. The USA has been particularly affected by such 'boomerang' scenarios. According to an important research group, the Federation of American Scientists, 'Past arms **exports** to governments and non-state actors in Panama, Haiti, Somalia, Iraq, Iran and especially Afghanistan have all turned into US security threats'.

Arms companies are more heavily supported by government money than most other **industries**. According to the Federation of American Scientists, US government support runs at US$ 6 billion annually – a third of the value of its total sales. Other leading arms exporters, such as Britain, France and Russia, **subsidize** their arms export industry too. This money could be spent on more important items.

**"Every gun that is made, every warship launched, every rocket fired represents, in the final analysis, a theft from those who hunger and are not fed, who are cold and are not clothed."**

Dwight D Eisenhower (US President, 1953–61)

Arms companies promote sales to poorer countries, which could be spending their money on water, sanitation, education and health programmes instead of arms. The **UN** classifies 46 countries as Least Developed Countries. Thirty of these are in Africa, where half the population – some 340 million people – lives on less than one US dollar a day.

Many governments that are arms buyers have alarming human rights records, and sometimes arms are used to violate human rights. In Iraq, US helicopters sold for crop spraying were used to attack Kurdish communities with chemical weapons. Continuing to sell arms to bad governments means their behaviour is being tolerated.

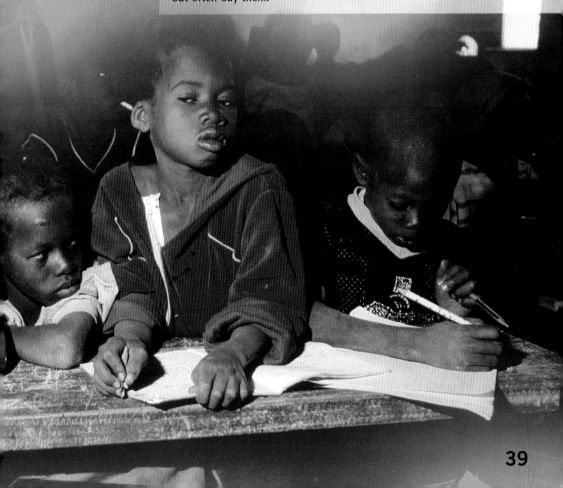

Children at school in Burkina Faso: education, along with other services, suffers in developing countries. They cannot afford arms but often buy them.

# What is being done to control the arms trade?

## The United Nations

The **UN** was established after the Second World War 'to maintain international peace and security' by developing 'friendly relations among nations'. Through its Department for Disarmament it takes action against the worst aspects of the trade. The department previously concentrated more upon chemical, biological and nuclear arms – but argues that increasing dangers come from small and conventional arms, which have become more widely distributed.

UN Headquarters in New York, USA.

## The UN at work

The UN held its first full-scale conference on the issue of small arms in 2001. Measures to remove guns from war zones when fighting is over were introduced. Wide-ranging ideas to prohibit private ownership of guns were unsuccessful. The conference agreed to meet again by 2006.

The UN sometimes imposes arms **embargoes**, which means it bans the sale of arms both into and from **conflict** zones. UN embargoes carry the **authority** of the international community, but the organization does not have the resources to police the arrangements; it relies on states to resist arms sales into those areas. There are countless examples of embargoes being broken. Throughout the 1990s, UN embargoes were placed on Angola, Liberia, Sierra Leone, Ethiopia, Eritrea, Yugoslavia and Afghanistan. However, private arms dealers, sometimes secretly assisted by governments who were keen to make money from old stocks, broke the rules and transported arms into these areas.

The UN Register of Conventional Arms was established after worldwide concern

UN peacekeeping
soldier in Cambodia.

at huge arms purchases by unstable countries, notably Iraq, which is ruled by a powerful dictator. The UN invited countries to declare how many weapons they buy and sell; it estimates that 90 per cent of global conventional arms sales are covered in the register. The UN believes too many arms 'pose a threat to national, regional and international peace and security'. If states were more open about the quantity of arms owned, they might appear less threatening – and others would then buy fewer arms.

Many people believe the UN's role is important. This is partly because the UN, by calling for **disarmament** measures, officially confirms that elements of the arms trade have caused international hazards. Campaigners hope that this will put moral pressure on individual governments to stop weapons leaving their own country. The most powerful part of the UN is the Security Council. Its five permanent members (USA, UK, France, Russia and China) produce up to 85 per cent of weapons bought in the world's arms trade. If arms sales are to be better controlled, the organization most likely to achieve the co-operation needed is the UN.

# Other international agreements

Various networks of international agreements have been set up to govern the arms trade. Some examples of these 'arms control' measures are given here.

## Small arms

The Economic Community of West African States (ECOWAS) made a three-year agreement in 1998 not to buy, sell or make any small arms. ECOWAS countries include Liberia and Sierra Leone – ravaged by civil war throughout the last decade. According to the **UN** 2 million lives were lost during the 1980s, due to **conflicts** and rebellions, and 7 million small arms were available in the region. This was the first agreement of its kind in the world. However, observers have challenged the effects of the agreement, saying that barely any Africans knew it existed. Ongoing conflicts in the region have driven the high demand for weapons.

## Conventional arms

The Ottawa Convention (1997) banned production, sale and use of anti-personnel landmines – explosives that are placed in the ground to destroy people. By the start of 2002 it had 142 signatories, although the USA, China and Russia – the largest producers and exporters of mines – have so far refused to sign. According to the US State Office, there are approximately 70 million anti-personnel mines buried in the ground of 70 countries, and 250 million mines in military stockpiles around the world. More positively, according to the UK charity Landmine Action, 29 countries including the UK, have reported they have destroyed their stocks.

Landmine victims in Cambodia.

# Weapons of mass destruction

The 1968 Non-Proliferation Treaty (NPT) was originally signed by the five official nuclear weapons states, and today has 187 signatories. Article 6 of the NPT ties signatories to make arrangements to end the nuclear **arms race** and eventually disarm their nuclear weapons. NPT states without nuclear weapons agree not to acquire them, and those with weapons agree not to transfer them.

The Chemical Weapons Convention has been signed by 144 countries, including the USA, Britain, Australia and New Zealand. The convention forbids making, storing, using and selling chemical weapons. The Biological Weapons Convention (1972) aims for the same with biological weapons.

There are limitations to these agreements. They all require individual countries to follow and police the rules, and some states do this better than others. This may be because they lack enough staff or money to police agreements effectively. Or it may be because governments simply choose not to follow the rules. However, most agree that the world is a far safer place with these agreements in place.

# Governments, NGOs and trade associations

Each country has its own set of laws controlling defence **exports**, which are made by national governments. However, some states may be less inclined to control where their arms sales end up than others. Because it is important to stop arms falling into the wrong hands, the **UN** is keen to introduce a basic standard of behaviour. There are many groups of people with different views seeking to influence politicians and decision-makers, at national and international levels.

Non-Governmental Organizations (NGOs) are independent of government. They have specialist knowledge of areas of social concern such as civil rights or arms trading. Some NGOs are extremely well known; for example, the human rights campaigning movement, Amnesty International claims to have around a million members and supporters in 162 countries. NGOs seek to change official behaviour through research and publications, advising politicians or

Sabine Christiansen
UNICEF-Botschafterin

Sir Peter Ustinov
UNICEF-Botschafter

A press conference for a UN Children's Emergency Fund (UNICEF) campaign to stop the production and trade of small arms.

celebrities, informing the media, recruiting new supporters, campaigns and public demonstrations. Large NGOs have good access to the media, national parliaments and international conferences. At the recent UN Conference on Small Arms an entire day was allocated to speakers from NGOs around the world, including the International Action Network on Small Arms (IANSA), Oxfam, Amnesty International with Human Rights Watch, and more regional groups – such as the Christian Council of Sierra Leone.

Delegates at an armed forces arms fair, where defence industries can display their latest products.

Workers and executives within the arms trade promote their concerns and interests too. The Australian Industry Group Defence Council promotes the 'positive contribution that Australia's defence industry makes to the Australian economy'. The UK's Defence Manufacturers Association represents the interests of 400,000 defence workers – of which around 20 per cent produce arms (defence) exports, while the bulk of the work is on projects for the UK Ministry of Defence. In the USA, the National Defense Industrial Association does the same for US workers from 950 companies producing military products. Such organizations advise parliaments and governments, provide briefings, give media interviews and sponsor defence exhibitions, research and publications.

The recommendations of defence associations are often (though not always) the opposite of those made by the NGOs. NGOs usually seek to introduce measures to reduce the arms trade, and therefore arms production, while trade associations seek to protect the jobs of their members.

# Getting involved

The arms trade is a deeply controversial global practice. For some it enables states and groups to defend themselves – when otherwise they could not. For others it feeds **conflict** and upholds the power of governments that behave badly to their peoples. At times it has been part of an **industry** that pioneers technology. On other occasions arms purchases wasted money in **developing countries** – where food, healthcare and education was badly needed.

What is clear is that the trade affects every one of us. More nations today have strong military capabilities that may one day endanger or save us. We may have relatives or friends who work in defence manufacturing plants that sell some of their products abroad. In cities around the world, or when visiting other countries as travellers, workers or peacekeepers, we may come across one of the 550 million guns in circulation. Many people live in war zones, and many more are refugees from areas where the availability of arms made it impossible to continue living there.

A good way to understand the complicated questions that the arms trade poses for different groups in society is to imagine the points of view of various people involved in the trade: for example, in the event of a conflict between two countries, what would an arms producer, an arms exporter, and someone who lived in a danger zone, be thinking? Group role-play can be a good way of taking the arguments forward: should arms sales continue as currently, or what changes could be made?

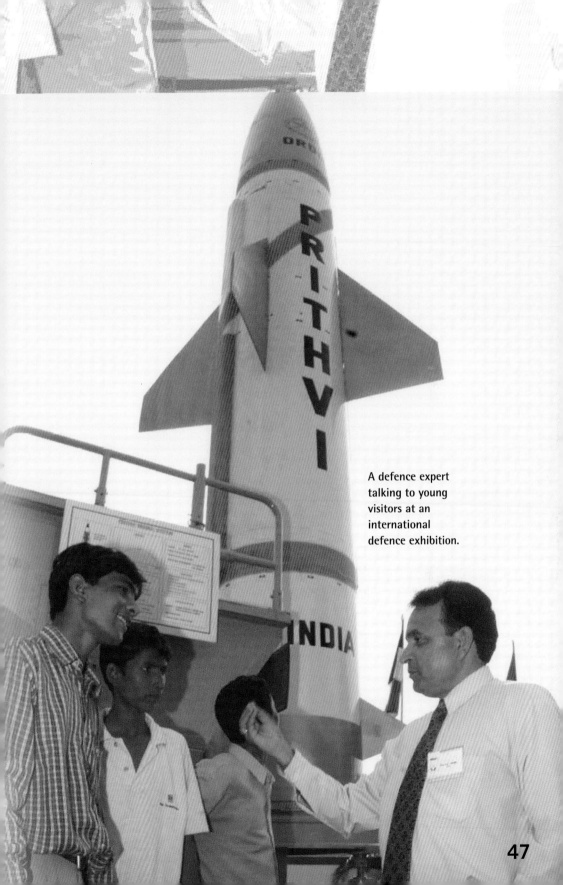

A defence expert talking to young visitors at an international defence exhibition.

47

Fighter jets returning from liberating
Kuwait after the Gulf War, 1991.

There are many ways to understand more and make your views known about arms trade issues. Sources of further information and contacts are given at the end of this book. The arms trade is constantly changing, so you should try to keep up to date with developments.

Other good sources of information are the Internet, and the serious daily and Sunday press although you should be aware that not all information available on the Internet is reliable. The foreign and financial pages of newspapers will inform you of large international arms deals – and areas of world tension.

Non-governmental organizations (NGOs) are often good sources of reports and information, although they are usually working against aspects of the arms trade. They are always looking for support and assistance. Their websites show what to expect in a campaign and the issues they are currently working on. Write or send an email to see whether there are any work-experience opportunities or supporter groups for young people.

Defence manufacturers also give information about their activities on their websites. Most of these companies also produce non-military equipment.

Another way to be actively involved is to write to your local MP or Congressman about a topical arms trade issue. Ministers are happy to hear the views of young people. You should receive an official letter back from them explaining their ideas and policies. Company representatives, local politicians, and people who work for NGOs will often visit schools to talk about their work.

The best way to see past and present military equipment safely is to visit the many military museums and air shows that are open to the public.

# Facts and figures

## Top ten arms buyers in the developing world (1993–2000)

| Rank | Country | US$ billions – imports | Region |
|------|---------|------------------------|--------|
| 1 | Saudi Arabia | 24.5 | Middle East |
| 2 | United Arab Emirates | 19.0 | Middle East |
| 3 | China | 12.6 | Asia |
| 4 | Egypt | 11.6 | Middle East |
| 5 | India | 11.5 | Asia |
| 6 | Israel | 9.5 | Asia |
| 7 | South Korea | 8.1 | Asia |
| 8 | Kuwait | 6.0 | Middle East |
| 9 | Pakistan | 5.3 | Asia |
| 10 | South Africa | 4.7 | Africa |

Source: CRS Report for Congress, CRS-48, August 2001

## Top ten arms companies globally

| Rank | Company | Home | US$ billions – arms sales |
|------|---------|------|----------------------------|
| 1 | Lockheed Martin | USA | 18.0 |
| 2 | Boeing | USA | 17.0 |
| 3 | Raytheon | USA | 14.0 |
| 4 | BAE Systems | UK | 13.2 |
| 5 | General Dynamics | USA | 6.5 |
| 6 | Northrop Grumman | USA | 5.6 |
| 7 | EADS | France | 4.6 |
| 8 | Thales | France | 4.3 |
| 9 | United Technologies | USA | 4.1 |
| 10 | TRW | USA | 4.0 |

Source: Defense News Top 100, 30 July 2001

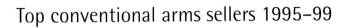

## Top conventional arms sellers 1995–99

| Rank | Country | US$ billions | Main customers |
|---|---|---|---|
| 1 | USA | 54.4 | Taiwan, Saudi Arabia, Egypt, Japan |
| 2 | Russia | 14.6 | China, India |
| 3 | France | 11.7 | Taiwan, UAE |
| 4 | UK | 7.3 | Saudi Arabia |
| 5 | Germany | 6.1 | Turkey, Greece |
| 6 | Netherlands | 2.2 | UAE, India, Greece |
| 7 | China | 2.2 | Malaysia, Myanmar |

Source: SIPRI Yearbook 2000

**Young girl with assault rifle, Cambodia.**

## Top small arms sellers

| Rank | Country | US$ millions |
|---|---|---|
| 1 | USA | Over 1,200 |
| 2 | Germany | 384 |
| 3 | Russia | 100-150 (estimated) |
| 4 | Brazil | 100-150 (estimated) |
| 5 | Austria | 60 |
| 6 | Czech Rep. | 59 |
| 7 | UK | 44 |
| 8 | South Korea | 43 |
| 9 | Sweden | 40 |
| 10 | Poland | 40 |

Source: Small Arms Survey 2001

# Further information

## Contacts in the UK

**Amnesty International UK**
99–119 Rosebery Avenue, London EC1R 4RE
Tel: 0207 814 6200
email: information@amnesty.org.uk
**www.amnesty.org**

**Campaign Against Arms Trade**
11 Goodwin St, London, N4 3HQ
Tel: 020 7281 0297
email: enquiries@caat.demon.co.uk
**http://www.caat.org.uk**

Lobbies to bring about the 'reduction and abolition' of the arms trade. International arms trade reports and two-monthly magazines on-line.

**The Coalition to Stop The Use of Child Soldiers**
PO Box 22696, London N4 3ZJ
email: info@child-soldiers.org
**http://www.child-soldiers.org**

Six NGOs provide a website giving questions and answers, campaigns and future events information.

**Defence Manufacturers Association (DMA)**
Marlborough House, Headley Road, Grayshott, Surrey GU26 6LG
Tel: 01428 607788
**http://the-dma.org.uk**

Topical issues in British arms manufacturing.

**International Action Network on Small Arms Transfers (IANSA)**
PO Box 422, London, UK, WC1E 7BS
Tel: 020 7523 2037
**http://www.iansa.org**

Network to prevent the increase and misuse of small arms. Information, diary and local contacts provided.

**Landmine Action**
1st floor, 89 Albert Embankment, London SE1 7TP
email: info@landmineaction.org
**www.landmineaction.org**

## Contacts in the USA

**Amnesty International USA**
322 8th Avenue, New York, NY 10001
Tel: (1) 212 807 8400
email: admin-us@aiusa.org
**www.amnesty.org**

**FAS Arms Sales Monitoring Project**
1717 K Street NW, Suite 209, Washington, DC 20036
**http://www.fas.org/asmp**

Federation of American Scientists (FAS), Arms Sales Monitoring Project – calls for 'restraint' in arms sales and runs one of the leading Internet sites with descriptions and pictures of weapons systems, and the trade trouble-spots.

**United Nations (UN)**
UN Headquarters, First Avenue at 46th Street New York, NY 10017
**http://www.un.org**

## Contacts in Australia and New Zealand

**Amnesty International Australia**
Locked Bag 23, Broadway, New South Wales 2007
Tel: (61) 2 92 17 76 00
email: adminaia@amnesty.org.au
**www.amnesty.org**

**Australian Industry Group Defence Council**
Australian Industry Group, Defence Council, GPO Box 817, Canberra 2601
**http://www.aigroup.asn.au/dmcindex.html**

Promotes defence industries and provides links to defence ministries around the world.

**Campaign Against Arms Trade (Australia)**
email: admin@acaat.org
**http://www.acaat.org**

**Amnesty International New Zealand**
PO Box 973, Wellington
email: campaign@amnesty.org.nz
**www.amnesty.org**

# Further reading

## REPORTS

**Human Rights Watch**
In-depth reports about human rights issues.
http://hrw.org/arms

**Norwegian Initiative on Small Arms Transfers (NISAT)**
Website with news reports from most countries about small arms issues.
http://nisat.org

**Defence Systems Daily**
Internet-based defence and aerospace daily news reports with free coverage of every region of the world.
http://defence-data.com

**Janes' Defence Army Technology**
Worldwide information on defence contracts. You can buy Janes' Defence Weekly in magazine edition.
http://janes.com/defence/

**Stockholm International Peace Research Institute (SIPRI)** researches international peace and security and publishes arms sales information on the website and in the SIPRI yearbook.
http://www.sipri.se

## BOOKS

*SIPRI Yearbook 2000, Armaments, Disarmament and International Security*
(Oxford University Press, 2000)
The world's leading guide to global military patterns.

*The Arms Bazaar in the Nineties: From Krupp to Saddam,* Anthony Sampson
(Coronet Books, 1991)
History of the arms trade told through stories about the companies that make arms, corruption scandals and the arming of Saddam Hussein in Iraq.

*Small Arms Survey 2000: Profiling the Problem*
(Oxford University Press, 2001)
Produced by Graduate Institute of International Studies in Geneva; profiles everything you need to know about the small arms trade in a factual, independent way.

# Glossary

**alliance**
a group of countries acting together

**arms race**
where one state buys arms and other states feel threatened and do the same

**authority**
person or organization's power to carry out certain actions

**bazaar**
market

**boomerang**
aboriginal tool that can return to the place it was thrown from; term used to describe an action that has unwelcome repercussions

**civilian**
not a member of any armed forces

**Cold War**
hostile relationship between America and the Soviet Union, so called because it never 'heated up' into direct war

**communist(s)**
people who believe the state should control production and distribution

**components**
parts that make up a final product

**conflict**
disagreement or war

**developing countries**
countries who do not have highly developed industry, and whose citizens are often poor

**disarmament**
reduction and abolition of weapons

**diverted**
when something is re-directed away from its intended route

**dual-use**
products for either military or civilian use

**embargo**
countries, regions or the UN make an order to stop the transfer of arms into or away from an area

**export licence**
a certificate from government granting permission to send equipment abroad

**exports**
goods sold abroad

**globalization**
where production and sales move beyond national boundaries and operate within a borderless world

**holocaust**
large-scale destruction

**import**
buy from abroad

**industry**
trade and manufacture, usually large scale

**legal (ly)**
permitted by governments and international law

**non-state actor**
rebel group

**reunification**
reunite separate territories, e.g. the joining together of East and West Germany in 1990

## sanctions
penalties for disobeying rules

## SIPRI
Stockholm International Peace Research Institute

## Soviet Union
from 1922–91, a block of fifteen republics controlled by its largest, Russia

## state-actor
government

## subsidize
when someone, e.g. government, pays for part or all of a project

## superpower
the USA and the Soviet Union (during the Cold War)

## surplus
amount left over after requirements are met

## 'sweetener'
favour or bribe given for particular decision

## Tsar
emperor of Russia (before 1917)

## UN
United Nations. An international organization of countries set up in 1945 to promote peace, security and international cooperation. The UN sometimes sends peacekeeping forces to areas in conflict.

# Index